Quick Guide to the Roman Forum

Including the Colosseum

Paul den Arend

Book design and production by VandiDesign
Editing by Paul den Arend

Published by: VandiDesign, Meerweg 112 9752 JL Haren, The
Netherlands

DEDICATION

This book is dedicated to the many people I guided through the Roman Forum and the Colosseum.

CONTENTS

1 Introduction

Visiting the Roman Forum is one of the highlights of any trip to Rome. This area was the heart of the Roman Empire. Here, the senate took decisions that affected people as far away as Britain and Syria. The Romans gathered here to hear news about the Empire. Triumphal processions took place here.

However, when you visit the Forum now, you find mostly piles of old stones. Without a good guidebook, you might even wonder why this place is so important. However, if you come well prepared and you know what you are looking at, the Roman Forum can come alive and your visit will be much more satisfying.

I am a tour guide and art historian, who has worked in Rome for many years. The forum is always one of my favorite destinations in Rome, because there are so many stories to tell about the temples, basilica's and arches. I hope this quick guide will help you enjoy the Forum as it should be enjoyed. It is a journey into the history of the Roman Empire.

2 The Roman Forum

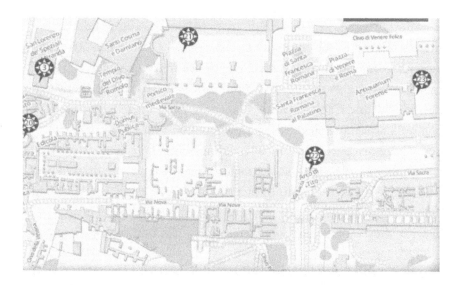

1 The Forum Romanum

Image 1 CC BY-SA 3.0 Wikimedia Commons

The Forum Romanum once was the heart of Rome. From the 6th century BC onward, this was the place where the most important public buildings stood. It was the political and social center of first the republic and then the empire. Forum means market in Latin, so it all started as the main market square of the city. Before, this area was a swamp. Archaeologists have discovered that the romans added 5 meters of sand to this area so it could be used as a market. Also, a very large drain was constructed, the cloaca maxima, which transported rain water directly to the Tiber. The forum lies between Palatine hill and Capitoline hill. Of course now not much is left. If you walk around without realizing where you stand it is not a very impressive place. Now, of most buildings only the foundations are left. In the middle ages and the renaissance this area was used like a quarry, like the Colosseum. In fact, if you enter a medieval church in Rome you can often notice how every pillar is different. This is because they were taken from different Roman buildings.

In Roman times this place must have been very impressive. This is where the senate building stood. There was a podium on which famous romans held speeches, like Cicero and Marc Anthony. Many temples and courthouses stood here. Roman writer Plautus described a normal day on the forum like this:

'If you need somebody for perjury, you should have a look at the area where meetings are held. Impostors and loud people you can find near the Temple of Cloacina. Rich folks that squander their money can be found in the shade of the hall of the market. There you can find withered prostitutes and all sorts of touts. In the lower market the rich citizens lounge around and on the middle forum, near the sewer you can see only posers.'

After the capital of the empire was moved to Constantinople the importance of the forum started decreasing. In the middle ages the center of the city moved northwest to the area near Piazza Navona. The place the forum used to be became known as the Campo Vacino, or the Cow's field. Only in the 19th century the first scientific excavations were started.

2 Basilica Aemilia

Image 2 by L.VII.C CC BY-SA 3.0 Wikimedia Commons

As you walk down you can see the foundation of the Basilica Aemilia on your right side. It was built in 197 BC. This building was meant to protect people from the rain or the sun. The activities that took place outside on the forum had to be continued on rainy days. it was some sort of trade center. Also, magistrates would hold trials here. That is also where the name comes from. Basilica comes from the Greek word *Basileus*, which means king. Of course, in ancient times it was the king who would administer justice. It was paid for by the Aemilia family, which was one of the most powerful families at that time.

It was destroyed in 410 by Alaric, the famous king of the Goths who sacked Rome. You probably know the word Basilica as a name for a church. This is because the first Christians used this type of construction for their first churches. The form of the classical temple was not suited to hold mass.

3 Temple of Antoninus and Faustina

Image 3 by Jean-Christophe BENOIST CC BY 2.5 Wikimedia Commons

This Temple is the Temple of Antoninus and Faustina. Antoninus is not a very famous Emperor. He was one of the adoptive Emperors. After Emperor Domitian became crazy and was murdered the senate decided that a new system for appointing Emperors had to be found. So they appointed one of their own, Nerva, Emperor. Nerva was not allowed to let his son be Emperor, but he had to adopt a promising young man as his successor. So Nerva adopted Trajan, who became one of the best Emperors, Trajan adopted Hadrian and Hadrian adopted Antoninus Pius. Antoninus is not very famous even though he was a very good Emperor. This is because during his reign nothing happened. The empire was at peace and a lot of people prospered. Antoninus then adopted Marcus Aurelius, who made his son Commodus Emperor. If you have ever seen the movie Gladiator you know that this did not work out very well.

This temple was built by Antoninus for his wife Faustina after she died. After his death it was dedicated to him as well. Emperors were always declared a god after they died. The Emperor who ordered the building of the Colosseum, Vespasian said some famous last words before he died. He said, Oh my, I think I am becoming a God. The building is still standing, unlike most buildings on the forum. This is because it was transformed into a church in the middle ages. In 1602 the building got a baroque facade.

4 Temple of Caesar

Image 4 by FrankCJones CC BY-SA 3.0 Wikimedia Commons

The Temple of Caesar was built in 29 BC by Emperor Augustus. This was the place where the body of Julius Caesar was burned after he had been murdered in the senate. You can walk inside and see a space which used to be an altar. On it you probably see flowers. This was the exact sport Caesar was burned. Still the romans remember him by putting flowers. On the 15th of March, the day Caesar died, flowers are put here, but also on other days.

Image 5 by Lalupa Wikimedia Commons

Image 6 by L.VII.C CC BY-SA 3.0 Wikimedia Commons

5 Temple of Castor and Pollux

Image 7 by Luiza CC BY 2.0 Wikimedia Commons

A little bit further you can see the Temple of Castor and Pollux. Only three Corinthian columns are still standing. It was built in 484 BC. Castor and Pollux were twins. Their father was Jupiter, who had seduced their mother Leda by taking the shape of a swan. Castor and Pollux were then born out of eggs. They were very important for the Romans. They believed the twins had helped them during an important battle against the Latin people at the lake of Regilius in 486 BC. After the battle 2 strong unknown warriors were seen on this spot, giving water to their horses. Afterwards these warriors disappeared but the Romans believed they had been Castor and Pollux. Then a temple was built on this spot.

The twins were not true gods, because their mother had been mortal. So when it turned out one died and the other one was immortal they were very sad. One was living in the underworld and the other one on earth. They wanted to stay together so their father put them as stars in heaven as the sign Gemini, twins.

6 The triumphal arch of Septimus Severus

Image 8 CC BY-SA 3.0 Wikimedia Commons

The triumphal arch of Septimus Severus was built in 203 AD in remembrance of his 10 years as Emperor and because of his victory against the Parthians. It was also dedicated to his sons Caracalla and Geta, but when Caracalla became Emperor he had his brother murdered and all references to his brother were taken down from the arch. You can see that there is a hole somewhere in the fourth line of the inscription. This is where Geta's name could be read. In the middle ages the arch stood half in the earth and a barber shop was run from under there. Caracalla's real name was Caesar Marcus Aurelius Antoninus Augustus Pius Felix but his nickname was Caracalla, which was the name of the Gallic Cape he always wore and made fashionable.

The area in front of the arch used to be the actual Forum, the market square. Only three trees stood here, they were a fig tree, an olive tree and a vine, which symbolized the essential foods of the Romans. Augustus had the forum paved with the travertine stones which you still can see.

7 The Forum

The area in front of the arch used to be the actual Forum, the market square. Only three trees stood here, they were a fig tree, an olive tree and a vine, which symbolized the essential foods of the Romans. Augustus had the forum paved with the travertine stones which you still can see.

8 Umbilicus Urbis

Image 9 by Karlheinz Meyer CC BY-SA 3.0 Wikimedia Commons

Next to the arch is the base of the Umbilicus Urbis. This spot marked the heart of the city, the bellybutton of Rome. You must have heard the expression 'All roads lead to Rome'. All roads lead to Rome and all those roads would lead to this point.

9 Curia

Image 10 CC BY-SA 3.0 Wikimedia Commons

This is the spot where the senate held its sessions. It once started with 100 senators, but in the time of Caesar there were 900. Emperor Augustus reduced their number to 600. The building burned down in 52 BC in the time of Julius Caesar. He paid for the restoration, but the senate was temporarily moved across town. So Caesar was not murdered on this spot, because at that time the building was being reconstructed. The present building is another reconstruction from the time of Diocletian in the 3rd century. Why do you think it is still standing? This is, as almost always with ancient constructions, because it was transformed into a church. Mussolini then changed it back to how it was before.

The senators sat on seats that were placed on the long side. Inside the Curia you can see Emperor Trajan's Plutei, fragments of the old stage in front of the Curia. On it you can a carving of the so called Suovetaurilia. This was a sacrifice in which a pig (sus), a sheep (ovis) and a bull (taurus) were offered. The bronze doors are copies, but the original ones still exist. Architect Borromini moved them to Saint John in Lateran, where they still are.

10 *Comitium*

The paved space in front of the Curia was the Comitium. The people of Rome would meet here to hold important meetings. Here, a long time ago, stood the Ficus Ruminalis. This was the fig tree on which the casket with Romulus and Remus had stopped while they were floating down the Tiber (remember the forum was a swamp before, connected to the river).

11 *Rostrum*

In the middle, in front of the actual forum, you can see the Rostrum. This used to be a stage on which important speeches were held. Marc Anthony held his famous speech here after Julius Caesar had been killed. What he exactly said is unknown to us, but many people know Shakespeare's rendition of the speech which starts with the famous words: Friends, Romans, Countrymen. Can you see the vertical lines on the front wall of the Rostra? Augustus had attached prows of the ships he had destroyed at the battle of Actium.

Cicero held many speeches here, including 14 very hostile speeches against Marc Anthony. He later took revenge by ordering the killing of Cicero and displaying his hands and head on the stage. It is said that more people came to see his head than had ever come to see his speeches.

12 Temple of Saturn

Image 11 by MarcoK CC BY-SA 3.0 Wikimedia Commons

Higher up you can see the Temple of Saturn. It is originally from the 5th century BC. This temple housed the treasury of the state. Also, weapons were kept here in case the Gauls would show up. Saturn was the father of Jupiter. He ruled as the highest god before him. He once heard a prophecy that one of his sons would one day take his place, so every time he fathered a son he would immediately eat him. Jupiter's mother was smart. Instead of giving Saturn his son to eat, she wrapped a stone in a cloth and Saturn ate the stone. He never found out, until Jupiter grew up and replaced him as Highest God.

13 Tabularium

Image 12 by Rita1234 CC BY-SA 3.0 Wikimedia Commons

This building once was the government archives. It was called the Tabularium. It was built on the slope of Capitoline hill. Big parts can still be visited, but from within the Capitoline museums. As you can see the lower part of the building is made out of ancient stones, but the upper part is more modern. This is because the modern city hall was built on top of the Tabularium in the renaissance.

14 Via Sacra

Image 13 CC BY-SA 3.0 Wikimedia Commons

The Via Sacra was the main road of the forum. Military and religious processions were held here who all ended at the temple of Jupiter on Capitoline hill. Many army leader and Emperor were welcomed here. If a victory was obtained someone could get a triumph. He was then allowed to hold a procession to show the spoils of war. Many barbarian kings were also shown to the people in chains or cages on this road.

15 Temple of Vespasian and Titus

Of the Temple of Vespasian and Titus only three Corinthian columns are left. Both Emperors were deified after their death. They were from the Flavian family and were responsible for the building of the Colosseum. It was a short-lived dynasty, because after Titus died his brother Domitian became Emperor and soon turned crazy with power. He was murdered and then the era of the adoptive Emperors started, with great Emperors like Trajan, Hadrian and Marcus Aurelius.

16 Basilica Iulia

Image 14 CC BY 2.0 Wikimedia Commons

Here you can see the foundations of the Basilica Iulia. It was paid for by Julius Caesar, who gave it his name. It was a courtroom and market and had two stories. Emperor Caligula once stood on the roof to throw golden coins at the people below. He liked watching people fight over money.

17 Lacus Curtius

Image 15 by MM CC BY-SA 3.0 Wikimedia Commons

The Lacus Curtius is the spot where the ground once split open during an earthquake. An oracle told the Romans the ground would only close if they threw in their most valued possession. A young man, Marcus Curtius, understood what the oracle meant and mounted his horse in full body armor and then jumped inside the hole. Of course young brave soldiers were Rome's most important possession. On this spot Emperor Galba was murdered.

18 Pillar of Phocas

In the middle of the Forum you can still see one pillar standing. This is the Pillar of Phocas. It was erected in honor of Emperor

Phocas, who gave the pantheon the Pope, who made it into a church, which is the reason it is still standing. The Pillar was taken from an older building, maybe the round Temple of Vesta which stands next to the Tiber, because that one misses a pillar.

19 Regia

Image 16 by sailko CC BY-SA 3.0 Wikimedia Commons

Here is the Regia. Once this was the place where the kings lived. After they were thrown out it became the residence of the Pontifex Maximus, the high priest. Pontifex Maximus means highest bridge builder, because the priest would build bridges between humans and gods.

20 Temple of Vesta

Image 17 by Tobias Helfrich CC BY-SA 2.5 Wikimedia Commons

Maybe you already noticed the Temple of Vesta. It is a small, round temple, that is still partially standing. In this temple the Vestal Virgins always kept a ceremonial flame burning. This flame was brought to Rome by Aeneas from Troy, the Romans believed. In their house, just behind the temple they also kept pure water. People that lived in Rome always could go to see the Vestal Virgins if they needed water or fire. When Rome was just a very small settlement the Vestal virgins already existed. They lived in a small wooden temple on palatine hill, which was also round, and provided the same service for the people of the village. The fire was once a year extinguished and started again by the Pontifex Maximus, the highest priest of the Roman empire. He was the only man who was allowed to enter the house. Inside the house you can still see some names of the virgins on the pedestals on which statues once stood.

The Pontifex Maximus chose six virgins. They were girls from patrician families and were between six and ten years old. After they joined the virgins their hair was cut and they were dressed in white. They then had to learn how to perform their duties for ten years, then they had to serve for ten years and the last ten years they had to teach the new girls how to be Vestal Virgins. After these thirty years they were free. They were not allowed any sexual contact. If they did, they were put to death by being buried alive. In the history of Rome this happened only ten times. But after the thirty years of service the Virgins were free and could also choose to lose their virginity if they wanted to, but most women preferred to stay alone, because they were used to being free. Women had very little rights when married.

The foundations of their house are still intact. This kind of building would later be used in the building of monasteries. You can see a courtyard; with around it cells where the Vestal virgins would live. In the middle was the basin where the pure water was held.

21 Basilica of Maxentius and Constantine

This huge structure is the Basilica of Maxentius and Constantine. It was started by Constantine's rival Emperor Maxentius in 308 and completed under Constantine. This building was the largest on the Forum. Half of it is still standing, the other half has disappeared. The roof was covered with gilded tiles, which were later used for the old Saint Peter's. The building was a Roman basilica, so it did not have a religious function. It served as courtroom and marketplace. Inside, in one of the niches, a huge statue of Constantine stood. The influence of this building has been enormous.

Many architects took inspiration from this building, especially renaissance artists like Bramante, Brunelleschi and Michelangelo. They came here and measured everything. They were really interested in the proportions of the build. You can clearly see the influence of this building in Saint Peter's Basilica, or for example in Raphael's fresco 'the school of Athens', inside the Vatican museums.

22 Arch of Titus

Image 18 by Daugirdas CC BY 2.5 Wikimedia commons

Down this road you can see the Arch of Titus. It was built in 81 AD in honor of Emperor Titus who had quelled the rebellion in Jerusalem and had conquered that city. He took the treasure of the Temple and on the arch you can see the kind of things he took. You can see a Jewish seven-armed candleholder, a menorah, for example. Traditionally Jewish people refused to walk under the arch, but now it's not possible for anyone to walk under it.

23 Temple of Venus and Roma

Image 19 by Khoogheem CC BY-SA 2.0 Wikimedia Commons

Here you can see the Temple of Venus and Roma. It was built in 135 AD under Emperor Hadrian, who might have designed it himself. He was an Emperor who was very much interested in the arts and had many buildings build throughout the empire. It was of course Hadrian who ordered the building of Hadrian's Wall in England to keep out the Scots. Also, the pantheon was built in this time. This temple was a bit of a break with the past. It looked completely different than other Roman temples. Hadrian loved Greece and Greek culture and experts can see a clear Greek influence in the layout of the temple.

24 The Mamertine Prison

The Mamertine Prison is located just outside the Forum, between the triumphal arch of Septimus Severus and Caesar's Forum. It is one of the oldest surviving prisons in the world. It dates from 64 BC and was mainly used to put prisoners who were sentenced to death. Gallic general Vercingetorix was decapitated here. When Nero was in power both Peter and Paul spent time in this

29

prison. Pope Sylvester I made it into a Church.

When Peter was locked inside this prison he begged his guards for water, but they refused to give him any. Peter then hit the floor three times with his cane and water appeared immediately from the floor. With this water he then proceeded to baptize his guards and cellmates. Petrus was liberated by an angel who cut his chains with his wings. There is a beautiful fresco of this scene by Raphael in the Vatican Museums.

3 The Forums of the Caesars

The area on both side of the Via dei Fori Imperiali are the Forums of the Caesars. As Rome grew the original forum became too small, so successive Emperors expanded the forum with their own ones.

Forum of Vespasian

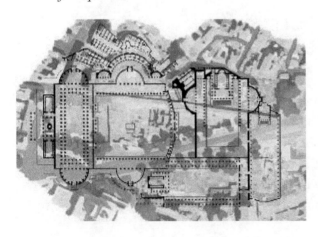

The forum of Vespasian is part of the imperial fora that Emperors build, because the Forum Romanum, the main market and square of Rome became too small. The remains of these fora can be found under the main *Via dei Fori Imperiali,* which was constructed under Mussolini. In the map above you can see this main road going across with a map of the old Imperial Fora over it. Big parts of the Imperial fora are buried under the street, but because the street is one of the main traffic arteries of Rome, it will stay under ground. Recently there has been a move to pedestrianize the *Via dei Fori Imperiali.* The idea is to make the biggest archeological park of Europe, including the Colosseum, Palatine Hill, the Forum Romanum and the Imperial Fora. So far only the traffic in the street has been reduced. Taxis and busses are still allowed to pass.

Image 20 by Nina Aldin Thune CC BY-SA 3.0 Wikimedia Commons

The Forum of Vespasian is almost completely gone. You still can visit the church of the Saints Cosma and Damiano, which was built inside what probably once was the library of the Forum. Inside this church you have a nice view of the temple of Romulus on the forum. You can also find some amazing early medieval mosaics here.

Forum of Nerva

Across the street some parts of the Forum of Nerva can be seen. Once, a nice temple of Minerva stood here. You can see all the forums are below the current level of the street. This is because during the last two millennia the city has become higher. You could call this due to the dust of ages. During the middle ages this area was not really used anymore. Cows were held here and slowly, thanks to dust and manure, the level of the ground rose considerably, until archeologist started digging in the 19th century.

Forum of Augustus

Image 21 CC BY-SA 3.0 Wikimedia Commons

Next to the forum of Nerva you can see what is left of the Forum of Augustus. He also built a temple in honor of the god of war Mars here when he won a battle against the murderers of Caesar, his adoptive father. Only three of the 24 columns are left.

Forum of Trajan

Image 22 by Zavijavah CC BY-SA 3.0 Wikimedia Commons

Here you can see the Forum of Trajan. Much of this amazing complex is still standing. Trajan was the first Emperor that was not from Rome. He was born in Spain, but from a family of Roman colonists. He was a promising young general when he was adopted by Emperor Nerva. He was a great strategist and won many wars. He conquered the Dacians, whom we now call the Romanians. He is the reason the Romanians still speak a Romance language and so many Romanians come to Italy to look for work. It is very easy for them to learn Italian.

Trajan also builds a lot of public buildings, like Vespasian and Titus before him. They also did not build a lot of buildings for themselves, because they wanted to consolidate their reign by pleasing the public.

Image 23 by Cezar Suceveanu CC BY-SA 4.0 Wikimedia Commons

Trajan's forum was finished in 113. He paid for it with the

money he made conquering the Dacians. The territory of the Dacians was filled with gold mines. He wanted to build the most impressive of Imperial Forums. His architect was the Apollodorus of Damascus, the most famous architect of that time. The most famous monument on his Forum is still standing. It is Trajan's Column. On the column you can see the story of Trajan's conquest of the Dacians in a spiral bas relief. Once the column was painted in bright colors, but now it is just white. It is almost 40 meters high (131 feet). The bas relief tells the story of Trajan's victory. It is a very interesting source for historians. You can see the Romans build bridges, set up camp and engaging in battle, all in a very realistic style. There are about 2500 figures visible and they are all of high artistic quality. Inside there are stairs which lead to the top.

On top there is now a statue of Saint Peter, which was put there to show Christianity goes above paganism. Originally there was a statue of Trajan there. After Trajan died, his ashes were held in a golden urn at the base of the column. According to a Roman legend, Trajan made it to heaven in the end, although he was never Christian. When Pope Gregory I the great visited the forum in the 6th century he looked at the column and saw a picture of Trajan comforting a woman who had lost her son. Gregory was deeply touched that he prayed for the soul of the deceased Emperor. His prayers were answered because he managed to bring the ashes temporarily back to life. He then baptized Trajan who could then enter heaven. The column is probably still standing because it was used as a bell tower for a medieval church, which now has long disappeared.

Behind the column you can see the actual forum. It was an enormous market and is still standing. It was basically a shopping mall. There were 150 shops on 6 floors. It is made out of brick, which had just been discovered. Downstairs probably dry foods like sugar and flour were sold and you could go upstairs to buy oil and wine. The medieval tower behind the forum is from the 13th century and is called the Torre delle Milizie. Soldiers were based here.

Forum of Caesar

Image 24 Ann Raia CC BY-SA 3.0 Wikimedia Commons

This area is the Forum of Caesar. You can see his statue standing in front of it on the side of the Via dei Fori Imperiali. He paid for this forum with the booty he captured in Gaul. In it was a temple to Venus. Caesar claimed his ancestry back to Venus.

4 The Colosseum

Image 25 by Diliff CC BY-SA 2.5 Wikimedia Commons

As long as the Colosseum exists Rome will exist. When the Colosseum will be destroyed, Rome will be destroyed and when Rome will be destroyed, the world will be destroyed'. These famous words were spoken by an English monk in the 8th century AD. It was also him, Beda Venerabilis, who was the first one to call the Colosseum Colosseum. The Romans never knew this building as the Colosseum; they called it something completely different. They knew it as the Flavian Amphitheatre. An Amphitheatre is basically a building which consists of two theatres put together. It was called Flavian after the name of the ruling family that constructed it. It was Emperor Vespasian, the first of the Flavian emperors, who had it built. He was the Emperor that managed to take power in the civil war that followed Nero's death. He had made his fame and fortune in Judea, modern Israel where he had stopped an uprising. When Vespasian took power he had to consolidate his reign. Nero, of course, had been crazy, but he was part of the first imperial family and could trace his ancestry back to the first emperor Augustus. Vespasian was not even from a very noble family. So to get the people to like him he constructed the Colosseum, right on top of Nero's enormous villa, the Domus Aurea.

Of course this was symbolic. Nero had built an enormous palace on the empty space that was created after the big fire, which destroyed half the city. Some people even whispered Nero had started the fire himself. He fiddled while Rome burned. Vespasian wanted to show that he was a very different emperor. He thought of the people instead of himself. So on top of the palace Nero built for himself a building was made for everybody to enjoy. The palace consisted of a big space where besides palaces there were lakes, forests and a zoo. The Colosseum now stands right on the spot where the artificial lake was.

So why do we call it the Colosseum then? This is because it got its name from a big statue that used to stand next to it. This was a huge statue of Nero. After Nero's death the head was changed to that of the Sun god. Everybody called the statue the Colossus. Then somewhere in the middle ages the statue was destroyed and the name got mixed up with that of the Colosseum.

Image 26 by Paolo Costa Baldi CC BY-SA 3.0 Wikimedia Commons

Most Roman cities had an Amphitheatre. The reason they were built is to keep the people happy. In Rome the people got Panem et Circenses or bread and circuses. This was to keep the populace quiet. You have to remember that a substantial part of the roman people were slaves. It was probably something like 40%. They did most of the work, so many of the one million people that lived in Rome did not have much to do. So sometimes they would rise up. Then the emperors started to provide them with free bread. A lot of grain was imported from Egypt. Then the people also got the games. Besides the fights of the gladiators and hunting games in the amphitheaters, they also got chariot races and theatrical plays, all for free.

The Colosseum was paid for with the money and valuables Vespasian's son Titus had taken from Jerusalem. Construction started in 72 AD. Most of the work was done by 12.000 Jewish slaves, all captured when Titus put down the insurrection in Judea. The exterior is remarkably well conserved, but inside not much is left. Many rocks and ornaments were stolen to build churches and other buildings in later times. The main structure is made out of concrete, a new invention at the time. The concrete was made from volcanic sand from the bay of Naples, mixed with water. Concrete was poured in wooden frames and therefore could take many shapes. The problem with concrete is it is quite ugly and needs protection from the elements. This is why many of the walls of the Colosseum were covered in marble stones. Of course this marble was later stolen to be reused or to be burned. A lot of marble was burned during the middle ages to make lime, which could be used to fertilize fields.

Can you see the holes outside the building? Many people think there was fighting here during a recent war, but the holes are there because there used to be iron inside them. With these iron hooks the marble was attached to the walls of the building. Later the marble was stolen, and also the iron could be reused.

Before it had four stories, but as you can see only in a small part the four stories are intact. If you would walk around the Colosseum would see that a big part of the outer ring is missing. For a long time the building was used as a stone quarry to provide building materials for the rest of the city. Many churches and palaces were built using stone from the Colosseum, like the Palazzo Farnese. The columns on the outside do not support the building, which is always the case in Greek building. They are just for decoration. Typically roman is the use of the capitals, the top part of the columns. You can see the three Greek orders of capitals above each other. The ground floor has Doric capitals; above that we see Ionian capitals and finally on the 3rd floor you can see Corinthian capitals.

Ludus Magnus

Image 27 by Jastrow Wikimedia Commons

If you would go up and cross the street you can see the remains of the Ludus Magnus. This was the training complex of the gladiators. It was connected to the Colosseum by an underground passageway.

Velarium

Image 28 by Jean-Léon Gérôme Wikimedia Commons

If you walk to the other side of the Colosseum you can see stones standing up next to it. These stones were used to tie ropes to. The Colosseum could be closed off to protect people from the sun and rain. The sunscreen was tied to these stones here. There always was a team of 100 sailors ready to close the arena with what they called the Velarium.

Gladiators

Image 29 by Russell Yarwood CC BY-SA 2.0 Wikimedia Commons

Now, what kind of games where played in the Colosseum? Of course, the fights of the gladiators were to most important part of a day at the Colosseum. These fights had a religious origin. Fights were organized at funerals. It was thought that the blood of prisoners could give deceased person strength on his trip to the underworld. But after a while these fights became very commercial. Rich magistrates would finance them to get support from the people. So after a few centuries the fights lost their religious context and became mass spectacles.

There were four schools for gladiators, which were called ludus in Latin. They had space for 2000 gladiators each. The gladiators were well treated because they were very valuable. First most of them were slaves or prisoners of war, but later a lot of people volunteered. If you were poor and a good fighter you could become famous and rich by risking your life in the arena. Gladiators could be stars like modern athletes.

A day in the Colosseum would start with hunting games. Many animals from all over the empire and further away died in the Colosseum. When the popes had the Colosseum cleaned and proclaimed a holy place, because of all the Christians that died there, a lot of very strange plants that did not grow in Italy were found. These came from the animal droppings. Many animals became extinct because of the Romans love for hunting games, like the North African elephant. When the Colosseum was opened in the year 80 during the reign of Emperor Titus, Vespasian's son, 900 wild animals were killed during 100 days. Below the arena there was a system of cages and cranes, which could make animals suddenly appear in the arena.

Do you know where the word arena comes from? Arena means sand, as it still does in Spanish. The arena was filled with sand to catch the blood of the animals and fighters.

The Colosseum was free and everybody could visit it. It had 80 entrances and if you walk around the Colosseum you can see numbers above every entrance. You would get a terracotta ticket with the number of you entrance and the number of your seat. It was a very efficient system. In 15 minutes everybody could enter or leave, which is impressing considering 50.000 people could fit in it.

Then, after the hunting games, there would be an intermission in which sometimes prisoners were executed. Many Christians died this way. The problem the romans had with the Christians was the fact that they recognized only one god. The romans considered the emperor also a god. So Christians refused to pay the proper respect to the emperor and the other state gods and this was considered like treason. So many Christians died in here and that is why it is now a holy place. Every year on Good Friday the pope comes here to remember them.

Arch of Constantine

Image 30 CC BY-SA 3.0 Wikimedia Commons

Next to the Colosseum you can see the triumphal arch which was built in honor of emperor Constantine. He was one the most important figures in western history. He was the first emperor that became Christian. Historians are not quite sure if he ever was baptized. Most people believe he was baptized just before dying, because the emperor thought it was impossible to be a good Christian and a good emperor at the same time. This is the last monument built in classical Rome, because emperor Constantine soon moved the capital to a new city on the Bosporus, which came to be known as Constantinople, now Istanbul.

Constantine became Christian because the day before an important battle he had a dream in which he saw a cross. An angel then told him 'In hoc signo vinces' or in this sign you will conquer. The next day Constantine ordered all his soldiers to paint crosses on their shield and of course he won the battle and became the sole emperor. Afterwards he started sponsoring Christianity. He ordered the building of Saint Peter's Basilica and Saint John of Lateran. He also presided over Church councils, like the one in Milan, in which Christianity was legalized. Constantine's influence was enormous. Before Constantine about 5% of the population of the empire was Christian, after Constantine about 60 to 70% of the population were Christian.

This arch was made by using parts of older arches, celebrating other emperors. Only the carvings just above the arches have something to do with Constantine. Elsewhere we see for example hunting scenes from the time of Hadrian. The inscription says 'The senate and the people of Rome devote this arch to Constantine, because he liberated the state from tyranny and infighting thanks to his godly inspiration and greatness of his mind.

Meta Sudans

Image 31 by David Jones CC BY 2.0 Wikimedia Commons

The Meta Sudans was the fountain where the victorious gladiators would wash the blood and sand from their bodies. The base of the Meta sudans can be seen in the above picture in the brown circular region just in front of the arch. Italian dictator Mussolini had most of it removed because it was standing in his way. He needed the space for military parades.

Colossus

Close to here, the Colossus stood: Now just a squared platform is left with a tree in the middle, but this is where the enormous statue of Nero stood, which gave its name to the Colosseum.

Palatine hill

Image 32 by Livioandronico2013 CC BY-SA 3.0 Wikimedia Commons

Behind the Arch you can see Palatine hill. This is one of the seven hills on which Rome was built and it was here that everything started. According to legend this was the place Romulus and Remus were nursed by the wolf. Romulus would go on and become Rome's first king, after murdering his brother. Afterwards this became the place where the emperors and noble families had their houses. This tradition was started by the first Emperor, Augustus, who built a relatively simple house on the hill, to associate him with the founder of Rome, Romulus. Later emperors built much bigger palaces on the hill. The English word palace comes from the word Palatinus. The hill is 50 meters high and archaeological evidence shows that the first settlement in this area was in fact on this hill, around 1000 BC.

The last Emperor of the Flavian family was Domitian, the brother of the well-loved Titus. He became crazy with power. He built an enormous palace on palatine hill overlooking the Forum and proclaimed himself a god during his lifetime. He was constantly afraid to be murdered, so he had the walls of his palace made out of polished marble, which had an effect like a mirror. This way he could always see if someone would sneak up behind him to kill him. In the end he was murdered in his bathroom, because there was no polished marble there.

Later emperors expanded Domitian's palace. It used to extend across Palatine hill and overlooked the Circus Maximus. The building of the part that is still visibly overlooking the circus was built during the reign of Septimus Severus at the beginning of the 3rd century.

ABOUT THE AUTHOR

Paul den Arend grew up in the Netherlands and has been travelling for most of his adult life. He studied art history in Salamanca, Spain, wrote reports for the Dutch Embassy in Santiago de Chile and studied Chinese in China. In between, he has been working as a tour guide. For many years he lived in Rome, Italy and guided groups of all backgrounds through the city. He has been a guide in the Vatican Museums, Saint Peter's and the Galleria Borghese, but he also loves to show groups around Sicily or Tuscany. His guidebooks reflect a profound love for the Eternal City and the many stories about its beautiful piazza's and landmarks.

Printed in the USA
CPSIA information can be obtained
at www.ICGtesting.com
LVHW011938230424
778112LV00021B/292